A Serial Killer: David Berkowitz
Son of Sam/Son of Hope

By

Stephen Cender and Kenneth Cender

Devil or Angel

David Berkowitz
Son of Sam /Son of Hope

The Original Writings From
The Son of Sam

Authors;
Stephen Cender
Kenneth Cender

ISBN: 1-58820-920-2

Copyright Reg. No. Txu 896-792 (02-20-98)

This book is printed on acid free paper.

1stBooks - rev. 01/24/01

David Berkowitz
Son of Sam a/k/a Son of Hope

Always the initiator of his own media, in 1997, hoping to convince the world that he is now a "born again christian", the Son of Sam sent a letter to the New York Daily News, and other similar publications, stating:

"The police and the news media used to call me the 'The Son of Sam', but God has given me a new name, 'The Son of Hope', because now my life is about hope… I am no longer the son of the devil."

In 1976 this serial killer initially received his name (The Son of Sam) from a long taunting note he left at the scene of one of his killings, and addressed to Captain Joseph Borreli who was publicized as a member of the Omega Team that was formed to hunt this psycho who was killing young women in various parts of the city with a .44 caliber handgun, stating:

"I am a monster, I am the Son of Sam."

Yet again in February of 1979 at a press conference that he called David Berkowitz, announced to the world that:

"The blood-thirsty Demons was just a concocted story invented by me in my own mind to condone what I was doing".

We must keep in mind that it has never been the police, nor the news media who had given David his different names. The psychiatrists tend to believe that David was delusional at the time he committed his crimes, and today, the religious community, dramatically and without an iota of questioning, tends to believe his claim to be born again in the persona of the Son of Hope.

In all instances, it has always been David Berkowitz who initiated press releases for his own reasons, and people who do not know him, nor have ever spoken to him, now proclaim HIS press releases as the TRUTH!

In a letter I received from David just prior to his "Son of Hope" press release, he tells me that:

"I am getting tired of all the negative publicity the press lays on me, and its about time that I created some positive publicity."

Approximately two weeks later, the press was filled with David's words as to how God came to him and gave him his new name; The Son of Hope.

In my (9) nine years of close association with David, as far as I am concerned, the book is still open as to whether or not he truly found God in his life.

While David surely comments in numerous letters to my brother and I, as to how he was grateful for encouraging him to write, my primary concern in getting him to write was to gain an insight into the mind of a serial killer, and hopefully, how we may learn to prevent similar occurrences in others nurturing similar traits.

Whatever we are to believe about this man, these definitive writings of his are his only true legacy. For better or for worse;

Welcome to the history of infamy, and into the mind of a serial killer.

Stephen Cender
Kenneth Cender

RELEASE

I hereby consent and release for use in advertising,
publicity, sale or publication in book or magazine form all
poetry and miscellaneous writings that I have given or sent to
Stephen Cender, and I waive all claims to compensation, monetary
or otherwise, for such use.

Description: <u>69 poems, various letters, short fiction, and</u>
<u>miscellaneous writings such as notes</u>

Signature _David Berkowitz_ Date _Jan 20, 1994_

Name (print) _David Berkovitz_

Address: _PO Box AG_

City: _Fallsburg_ State: _New York_ Zip: _12733_

Witness Signature _Kenneth Cander_

Witness Name (print) _Kenneth Cander_

Address _P.O. Box AG Fallsburg N.Y. 12733-0116_

Mr. Stephen Cender
265 Mill Road,
Staten Island, New York
10306   December 7, 1989

Dear Steve:

        When I first came to prison I thought that I
would never survive this ordeal. For years I languished
in a prison cell accomplishing nothing, wasting away.
But then - I believe it was in 1981 - I first met you
and your brother Kenny. Both of you, although you
were confined like me, had a sense of direction and
purpose. You and Kenny read voraciously, always
had a book in your hands. I noticed too that you
both had a vision of something better, and your
many prisoners' rights projects certainly proved
this.

        It was you and Kenny, Steve, whether you
realized it or not, who provided the inspiration
for me to do something positive with my life.
You encouraged me to write, and you stood by me
until my pen got moving.

        Within the last few years I have written some
poetry, mainly prose, and a few short stories. I have
fallen in love with words, it seems. And this love
affair originates with you and Kenny. Therefore, I
am giving to you my entire collection of poems and
other miscellaneous writings. You may do with
these as you please, as you see fit.

        You said that you like some of my work. Well
thank you. My father says the same thing. But per-
sonally, I think they are poor excuses for poems.
Of course I'm only a novice with little education,
and almost no education in the fine arts. There's
a big mountain yet to climb. But with you and
Kenny pushing me, who knows, I may have a future
after all.

I hope you enjoy reading these poems as much as I enjoyed writing them. Words are a mystery to me and an adventure. Even if these writings are of little merit, I still enjoyed the total experience of putting them together.

Thank you for your help. These poems are a gift of soughts. Good luck to you with your life. My one request is that you look out for my elderly father in any way that you can. He's proud of my going back to school and of what I've managed to do with a pen. Thanks again for the encouragement.

Best regards,

David Berkowitz

THE WINE MAN

Here comes Walter the Wine man
Lugging a pail of juice that's
Sour as a bitter lemon,
Red as a can of paint,
Smelling like burning tar-
Tasting like turpentine
Roasted in the hot summer sun.

'Who'll buy a cup of this brew
That I've carefully prepared?
Nursed to perfection and
Better than the finest port
Money can get-
Sweeter than the finest grapes
From the Italian shore.

"Made under strict supervision,
And with the greatest skill,
In a broom closet
By the carpentry shop
In the basement
Of cell block "D"

"For a pack of cigarettes
You'll get a cup
Of the best wine
You've ever tasted-
Elegant, exquisite, unique-
The choicest in the land.
"Come with me, Dirty Walter,
And satisfy your soul.
Tell me, have you ever tasted
Wine like this?
Drink! Drink to forget
Your misery and troubles,
If only for today!"

David Berkowitz

April 23 1986

MUSCATEL MEDICINE

Here's a story I've just got to tell.
Its about a poor old man
And his bottle of Muscatel.

Never has a friend been so near.
Never has such a thing been so dear.
Never has a cure been found
For all the heartache that's around,
As my ole Muscatel.

I've always been poor.
And I just know
I ain't gonna be much more.
I struggle daily to make ends meet.
Just an ordinary fella
Whose tasted nothing but defeat.

But one thing's for sure.
I've found the cure
For all my troubles,
And all my woes.
It's a cure that
Few have had
The privilege to know.
Its called Muscatel,
And it works very well.

Oh sweet Muscatel!
I know you're taste so well.
A life full of sorrow, bitterness
And woe.
Save for you, where else can I go?

At times life is a living hell.
But alas,
My dear friend Muscatel.

David Berkowitz

April 25, 1986

To My Friends! Here is a poem I wrote.

They Meet at Night

They meet at night
When the world is dark
And the owl stalks its prey.

They meet at night
To seek the Voice
Of the Prince who hates the Day.

While saints sleep

The black cats creep

Scent of blood everywhere.

Music sensuous

Bodies dancing

Virgins in despair.

Then at sunrise

Saints awaken

No trace of Darkness anywhere.

Daniel Berkowitz
"Son of Sam"
Sept. 8, 1988

3

I wrote the following poem on August 16, 1988.
I am not quite satisfied with it and it will
need some revisions.

On the Train to Treblinka

My neighbors and I have never been so close
Elbow to elbow
Nose to nose
Cattle cars rattling
The night sky is getting dark
Not a star can be seen
A forbidding Omen?

The smell of fear is everywhere
Instincts know
The towns and cities left behind
The children who will never grow

Fate uncertain
A sense of doom
Are we really the "cancer of the earth"?
Or are they just deluded Knights of War?
The Nazis.

The air is sweet and cool
Filtering through the cars
Rich farmland
Fertile soil
Organic farmers, all of them
I wonder what they use for fertilizer?

Sunset coming
The night is ready to begin
Just in time for supper, I hope
Our cars are coming in.

Ah, we're stopped!
We're here!
Journeys end
Soldiers yelling
The moans of the prisoners.

Look!
They're letting us go free.
The doors are opening and out we come
Fresh air hits my face

How beautiful is this place
Buildings new and modern
Manicured lawns, and flowers in bloom
Birds in the trees singing
And a band of teenagers are playing a popular tune.

Songs of welcome greet my ears
The moans of pain dying out
"Ah," says a German soldier
His brass buttons gleaming in the twilight
"Care for a nice shower to refresh your soul?"
"Yes, splendid!
"Please show me the way, sir."

up the narrow path I travel
Pushing and shoving from those
Waiting to get clean.

So this is Treblinka
An efficient camp indeed.

by David Berkowitz
april 22, 1989

Man On Fire

The acrid smell was first noticed by Alice Klump, the head secretary for the accounting department. Her keen nose sniffed the air for its point of origin. "Gosh that stinks," said Alice to her neighbor, Hazel Cobble.

Known more commonly to her office coworkers as "Fat Hazel," she too noticed the awful odor. The fat lady, her tremendous girth resting fully in her extra-padded chair, blurted out, "It smells like burning flesh!" And, as it turned out, Fat Hazel was right.

Seconds later, a piercing scream filled the air. The door to Mr. Jackson's office burst open, and out he came, his hair a ball of fire. To add to the shock of it all, in his right hand he held a shiny hammer, and he was beating himself about the head with it.

Quick thinking Alice leaped off her chair and ran to the water cooler with her drinking cup. As for Fat Hazel — you never saw a 380-pound hippo move so fast. Within a millisecond she was off her chair and running down the office corridor. Her bouncing body set coffee cups rattling and paintings falling from walls.

Unfortunately for Mr. Jackson, he would not survive the ordeal even though the blaze was extinguished within minutes by a platoon of secretaries using mugs filled with cold coffee.

Then, as the tearful office staff gathered around the body of their accounting department head, his hair still smoldering, a blue cloud began to appear in their midst. In an instant it formed into a man.

He looked like an ancient sage coming out

of a time warp. His garments gave him a Buddha-like appearance; his voice was like that of a prophet's.

Before a stunned and silent audience, he began to speak. "Ah my friends, this is a lesson from the fox," he said. "How so?" said Mrs. Tupper, her face frowning with uncertainty.

"Well you see, ladies, the fox is a sly and intelligent animal. He is quite cunning and always seems to outwit the chicken farmer. Yet, when pursued by hunting dogs, the fox is easily confused. In a panic, it runs in circles, then drops from exhaustion. To be a fox in business is to invite defeat."

"So what does this have to do with Mr. Jackson?" asked Elsie Klingstein. "Ah," said the sage, "your boss was being pursued by others above him. Confusion produced stress, and the stress was

9

causing the internal temperature inside his brain to increase, hence the fire."

"But why was he using the hammer?" said Hazel Cobble, her fat buttocks pressing against a nearby wall for support. "Ah," replied the sage again, he did not know where to aim the eyes."

"Now what's this supposed to mean?" asked Gilda Smith, the youngest member of the office. The sage easily explained: "When you look at things with your eyes, the eyes give birth to illusion. No one thing looks the same to each person. I'm afraid your boss viewed his problem incorrectly. He would have been wise to look at his business through the Eyes of the Mind. Each individual must look at the world through the Eyes of the Mind in order to see everything in its proper perspective. These eyes do not deceive. But our physical eyes often see things that are not there, like a mirage in the desert."

New immediately after he spoke these words, he vanished into the air. Everyone in the office remained motionless. The experiences of these last few minutes left them numb. Fat Hazel, however, was the first to speak. "I'm glad he's gone," she said. "It's lunch time, and I'm starved." Taking her cue, the rest of the workers quickly regained their equilibrium and charged towards the cafeteria.

by David Berkowitz
April 21, 1989

I wrote this poem on August 20, 1988 while being forced to choke on cigarette smoke. I was very angry when I wrote this, and I'm still angry!

The White Death Stick

Epoch of Death
Thou foul breathing monster
Carbon soot
And ash rain dew
Blue hue cloud
Of volcanic disaster
Alabaster greyish stew.

Yellowed fingers
Of encrusted plaster
Teeth blackish this doth shew
Evil eyes of bright red sparkles
Odor of burning shrew.

-Continued-

Flesh distasteful
Foul complexion
Stink of burning eschewing you.

Patsy patron of capitalist fools
Poison so perverse
Porcine of blue
Cancerous ball of iron long crust
Death is lurking
You smell of disgust.

You miserable glutton of white stick cancer
Die already!

You foul reeking polluter of my heaven,
Die!

Oh clean air
I long to suckle thy bosom
Let me breathe God's gift.

by David Berkowitz
composed August 20, 1988
written April 22, 1989

13

The Adventures of Mr. Finkelstein

"Son of a bitch!" mumbled an irate Melvin Finkelstein to himself. "All these damn flies!" He bent over his bowl of split pea soup, and with his spoon, he gingerly scooped the squirming insect out of the green muck.

On a napkin beside the bowl he had amassed a sizeable collection of fourteen flies, all gathered in a matter of minutes. And all of them intruders to his lunch. None of these critters were going anywhere. Once the thick soup began to dry, its effect was like glue.

"I'm going to find the manager of this place," swore Finkelstein to himself. "These damn flies are everywhere." And they were. Scanning the people at their tables, it seemed as if the bugs had invaded every customer, with no exceptions. Flies brazenly walked across sandwiches, hamburgers, and people alike. Yet to Melvin's amazement, no one but himself seemed to be annoyed.

Angry and disgusted as the fifteenth fly just invited itself for a swim, he flung his spoon down onto the formica tabletop; it made a loud "clink" when it hit. And off he went in search of the manager, all the while mumbling curses under his breath.

Jack Sherman, the restaurant manager, was not hard to find. For he sat twenty feet above the crowd in what appeared to be a lifeguard's perch. Above him was a huge billboard sign that said, "I'm The MANAgER — So What's Your Complaint?"

Finkelstein waved up to him to get his attention. In a flash Mr. Sherman jumped off his seat, slid down a shiny brass pole like a fireman, and in the blink of on eye was standing before his dumbfounded customer.

"What the heck do you want?" asked Sherman. "Listen," said Melvin, "I just fished fourteen flies out of my soup, and a fifteenth swimmer is busy doing the backstroke."

Once started, Finkelstein couldn't stop talking. What was going to be a simple complaint turned out to be a long, carping denunciation of his life as a real estate salesman.

"I'm worthless," sobbed Finkelstein as flies danced across his face, exploring salty tears. A sympathetic Sherman listened politely.

"You know, I haven't made a sale in three years. I even tried to sell on abandon mansion to a homeless family for one dollar. The place was in mint condition, and I blew the deal!" lamented Finkelstein.

"In fact, I have an old Civil War cannon at home; a relic that once belonged to my great-grandfather. There's a stack of cannon balls to go with it. Once I was even contemplating suicide by loading a ball, lighting the fuse, then standing in front of it."

"Well," said the manager, "have you tried flies?" "Flies?" "Sure," said Sherman. "Perhaps you should go into the fly business. It's a growing market, and there's no risk at all."

Sherman continued his explanation: "I grew tired of the dishwashers we have here. These bums were lazy. They never changed the water and the dishes were always encrusted with old food. The customers were complaining. So I fired them and replaced the dishwashers with flies. Since the Federation of Free Flies gives out flies for free, it cost me nothing. In fact, I saved lots of money."

17

"Now these flies," Sherman went on, "they work on the batter system. The customers leave behind their uneaten scraps. Then my flies zoom in, devour what's left, and lick the dishes and utensils clean. When the next customers go to sit down, they see sparkling clean plates.

"The only draw back is that some of these cleaners get a little greedy and start on a meal before a customer is done."

"Look," said Sherman, "why don't I start you off in the business." "Oh no," said Finkelstein, "I don't want you to stick your neck out for me." "No problem," the manager said. "There's no capital required."

Mister Sherman reached down behind the counter and pulled out a large coffee can. "Here, you can have these for a starter," said the manager. "There's about two thousand flies in this one. When you're ready, you just pop de lid and let them go to work."

"Say you know something, Sherman, I think you did me a big favor here. I've made my decision. To hell with real estate. I'm gonna go flies.

"In fact," added Finkelstein, "this first one will be a gift for my wife. For years she's been bugging me about a dishwasher. We could never afford one. And next week its her birthday.

"Boy, will I surprise her tonight," remarked the joyous man. "Right after supper they'll be a big stack of dirty dishes. When she starts to head for the sink, i'll say, wait honey! I've got you some help for the kitchen. Then i'll pop the lid, and before you know it, several thousand flies will be busy at work, licking every dish sparkling clean."

"Sherman," Finkelstein added, "all my life I've been on utter failure. Even my marriage was going down the tubes. But with this can of flies, I think that my wife will begin to look at me in a different light."

With his can of flies, a happy Finkelstein went out the door of the restaurant. He felt confident now. His marriage was going to be saved, he believed. And he was embarking on a new career.

***End ***

David Berkowitz
4/27/89

And The Headlines Read:
Only Child Dies — Suicide!

Child most loved
Blessed from above
Joyful at his birth
Parents whose lives
Were filled with mirth.

All their hopes
Were invested in him
All their dreams were
Now to come true
The desire of a lifetime.

But the world
Is full of mysteries
And forces that know
No bounds
Had other plans.

The dreams were gone
And disappearing was that hope
Death and destruction found
A dupe to carry on their work
And all the joy died with him.

by David Berkowitz
May 1, 1989

Dead Son Proud Dad

by David Berkowitz
May 10, 1989

I remember being born
That small house neat and cozy
Momma always had an apron on
Her hair done in a bun
Daddy was a plumber
And we lived in Pittsburgh —
Still do.

I wasn't much in school
Hated it and preferred to work
On cars or chase chicks
Drag racing for fun
What else was an All-American
Middle class boy to do —
Dull life.

My daddy was a veteran (WW II)
Mom shipped him packages of cookies
To Germany before they were married
Dad said he once shot a Nazi soldier
And stories about the war filled our home
So even before I went I was —
A Vet.

23

John Wayne taught me
About Shooting Japs
I had my own guns
A .22, A BB-rifle, And
A water pistol from first grade
So I knew All about killing —
G.I. Joe.

In 1969 I knew that
The commies were overrunning
Vietnam — Never heard of this
Place before —
It was my turn And
Dad And John Wayne were both —
Very proud.

Wearing my uniform — Age 19 —
I was At one with the universe
Going to War like daddy
All the Pittsburgh Steel workers
Would drink to that —
Boy Soldier.

T.V. Fantasies of war died
When I tasted my own blood
Screaming in pain
Where's John Wayne
To save me in the nick of time
Sweet Jesus this is real —
I'm dying.

Daddy's son died at
Dak Toe Delta
Twelve clicks east of Dong Duc
At home momma wears her apron
And daddy flies the National colors
On D-Day — Son Age 19 —
At Death.

— End —

The Penitent in Sanctuary

by David Berkowitz
May 10, 1989

Cold concrete, dank and damp
Dark corridors with muffled
Echoes of footsteps
Only candles illuminate the
Ghosts of desire.

Hushed silence upon dewy walls
Endless chambers and distant
Celestial bells
Harken all callers onto Thee.

Deepest wells of pristine solitude
Shadowed by iron black cisterns
To catch drops of rainwater
Trickling down meandering cracks.

Censers with cherubic faces
Line eternal caves
Denoted by Celtic crosses in
Front of tiny, barren cells
A small woolen mat to mark
A bed.

Casks of dark purple brew
In cellars while forbidding
Chants and chimes haunt
These sons of perdition
A dreamer's paradise of
Penance and contrition.

Penniless from lack of want
Valedictions, please, for all
Who've entered her doorways
And penetrated her murky depths.

The Supreme Sacrifice

by Daniel Berkowitz
May 11, 1989

Here I am
Dead man's carcass
Flies exploring the holes
That were once my eyes
While blood quenched
The thirst of a hungry
Earth.

You sit unmoved by my
Sacrifice
Sipping cherry Kool-Aid on ice
On your patio floor watching
A ball game
Hot dogs sizzling on a charcoal
Grill.

I screamed in pain
Body trembling with hurt
While my mind flashes
A thousand thoughts of Paradise.

You mowed your lawn
And eyed your sleek two
Cars with pride
T.V., Stereo, Video all playing
The National Anthem
While your children toyed
With intergalactic soldiers
From Mattel.

You weren't with me
When I climbed those mountains
Searching for him who'd deprive
You of all your belongings
If you'd but let him
March up your street
Calling cadences for Uncle Ho.

Ten thousand miles away
I fired my gun to the
Tune of Dixie
While my legs danced
Involuntarily at impact
Of AK-47 7.62mm
But you couldn't see me,
Of course
For I was camouflaged

↓

29

And your head
Was buried in the Sunday News.

I Lie still now
Putrid smell of corpse decaying green —
Remember me on Memorial Day
When you eat your steak in peace
Bright red roses growing in your
Garden.

-End-

The Guru

by David Berkowitz

May 12, 1989

If you'd but believe......

Allow me to show you a day
That is unlike any other,
An adventure in space
Where celestial beings
March at my pace.

The world has had enough of violence
Let us begin anew to create
Life from above
For I command you to love
Mother and brother.

31

Let us dance with the angels of heaven
And with all of our brethren
Who have gone on before
To that distant shore
For we desire their help
All the more.

If you'd but believe that I Am He —
Then on this we will agree.

A Case of Demon Possession

You don't remember when it happened,
But I do ......

Once while you were sleeping
And you were dreaming
I approached your bed creeping
And I was peeping
On such a dark night
Surely the blackest night of the year
I crept into your body
Ever so gently
And stole your soul
And took control

Like a pilot in the cockpit
I fueled the fires
of hatred and retribution
upon an ignorant world

Friends at birth
(For I watched you coming into the world)
Friends for life
(Yet you don't know my name)
Your body and soul
Are to me like man and wife

We're married now
Our union complete
You're all mine
And I'm in the driver's seat.

by
David Berkowitz
May 13, 1989

I Remember Grandpa

So long ago
Just a blur
You held me
Made me laugh
Always a smile
A happy time
I won't forget

Your fine pennies
Your wet kisses
Your prickly whiskers
Before God came
To take you
To the graveyard.

-by-
David Berkowitz
June 22, 1989

The Passing

"You are just a vapor that appears
for a little while and then vanishes
away."   St. James 4:14b

God called your number and you were gone

Like a lark speeding towards its nighttime nest

You've vanished leaving all your work undone

North by west your soul flew off into

The sunset

Nimbus light fading

Your aura growing dim

i'll always remember you, brief dreamer

Though our chances of meeting again

Are very slim.

-by-
David Berkowitz
June 27, 1989

Sylvia

Madness held you tightly in his hands.
We all knew that he would one day find you
No matter what personality you tried to
Hide in.

He had stalked you from your birth,
Singling you out from among the many.
Neither marriage nor motherhood could
Save you from his net.

Your hair matted and stringy,
And your face covered with soot
Reveal the wounds of psychotic
Battle.

One nervous breakdown after another
Succeeded in driving you to him.
A true martyr,
You were betrayed by many.

Slipping out by gas,
You left for the nether world
To join the dead,
To visit your father.

Your ghost still haunts the poets of
renown, and your work is left undone.
Woman of schizophrenic torment, may the
Angels light a path for you to follow.

Remember, "Even amidst fierce flames,
The golden lotus can be planted."

by David Berkowitz
June 23, 1989

The F Train

Squeezing through X-shaped spindles
In damp dark airless caverns,
The underground Warrior
Girds up his loins for
The coming battle.

Soldier of fortune in that
Steel cave,
Sweat dripping as
Maiming-point, sharp-tipped umbrellas
Stab at his eyes.

A sea of anger-blank faces
Swarm before him, unrelenting.
His legs bloody from
A thousand kicks.
Shirt torn and shredded.

Schools of piranha in suits
Drip their saliva upon
His worn fingers gnawed to
Fragments by razor-sharp teeth -
An ugly grin greets him with wine smell.

Heart palpitations from rattled nerves,
Underground warrior challenges all comers
For his royal seat, a throne
Of oily grime-greased plastic
In a New York City subway car.

Rush hour commando,
His attaché case a shield
Staves off attack wave squads
Of raving men and women
Vying for a steel horsey ride home.

David Berkowitz
June 25, 1989

Over The Old Stone Wall

Over on a distant shore
Lies a land flowing with milk and honey,
And so much more.

Here nothing lives, only dies —
Broken hearts, and watery eyes.

Peace of mind is never known,
Crowds of men, yet all are alone.

When I awake to the morning hell,
my cell door opens to the gates
of hell.

Another day, another cry —
Sometimes I just long to die.

Over on that distant shore,
There is a promise of something
more.

41

A hope that fades is no hope at all.
But I know there is a land on the
other side, of the great wall.

Perhaps one day when the gales are
strong
I'll put up my sails and sail right
around that old stone wall.

David Berkowitz
July 10, 1989

Extinct

The strongest species of the Kingdom is
dying
The cunning animal is being crushed
daily
The spiritual man is drifting into
decadence

Men in transition
New urban beings
City slickers
Corrupt and crippled

Domesticated man
Herd men
Sick men

Bone weary creatures
Caricatures of what
Once was strong

Weakened workers
Civil servants
Model citizens

Slow breathing
Half dead sufferers
With instincts asleep

Urban men
Grinding out daily chores
Devoid of dreams

The woodsmen are dead
The bird watchers extinct
Smog choked
A sick god stalks the cities.

David Berkowitz
October 4, 1989

The Creature That Was Man

dinosaur brained
domesticated man
marching with
the herd
on pavement
trails
tired, sickly
bone weary
creature
caricature of
what was
once strong
proud, alive
Now dying
Weakened worker
Slow breathing
Half dead
instincts asleep
grinding out
daily chores

devoid of
dreams
carbon lunged
Ozone victim
soon will
be extinct

David Berkowitz
October 5, 1989

Inconsiderate Smoker

Scarred lung cougher
Channels toxic soot
Carbon chemical cannibal who
Chokes little kids

Insidious imp
Sends smoke signals
To his comrades
Sitting across the room

"Lets attack now;
Smother them swiftly
With our noxious fumes.
This is Ozone Warfare!"

Smirking soldier with his
Tobacco stained face
Refuses the ashtray
Shuns any truce.

Self-indulgent warrior he
Cradles his cigarette lighter
Like a madman
With a gun.

David Berkowitz
October 5, 1989

Fragments

What can we do
But pity a tarnished life
Of immoral conquests
And failed dreams
Empty of merriment
Of a yearning for
Hearth and fireplace
Wife and love
Everything now in
Fragments

David Berkowitz
October 6, 1989

49

Nature Call

I heard that call again, I did
Deep within my soul, amid
Cries of loons
And woodcock tunes

Moors and swamps
Dressed in cattail browns
Foxtail ornaments
With foxfire crowns

Dark at night the only sound
A hissing of nature spites
In the ground
And hidden dandelion kings
Whisper at being clothed
Yellow, red, brown

A humming bird with a sing-song tune
croons, croons, croons
while shrouds of evergreen jeweled shrubs
Dance under a cloudless moon.

David Berkowitz

Oct. 11, 1989

The Wandering Minstrel

The pious hermit
and wandering minstrel
will sing his sad song
for only a nickel

with warped guitar
this one tarnished star
a vagabond in
tattered vestiments
struggles against
the elements

clothing ripped and out-worn
tells of a tale now ended
of a dream once born

David Berkowitz
October 12, 1989

Anne Frank Says,
"Never Again"

I sleep gentle
I sleep sweet
I sleep in a lime pit
Six feet deep

my brothers to the left
And my sisters to the right
Never Again to see the sunset
Never Again to see the night

No cross to mark my grave
No headstone granite grey
No angel picture
No flower pot

Nor a mound of clay

This is the Nazi way,
You see
To hang Jewish kids
Like me

David Berkowitz
oct. 15, 1989

53

Into Eden

Into this Eden he came
We thought he was seeking glory and fame
A mountain man with a strong hand
We hoped he'd tame this savage land
. . . .

But really,
He says he just came here to be alone.

Daniel Berkowitz
October 21, 1989

Cancer Cell

I'm just one
But I can make many
I'm just one
But I can make trouble plenty

If I go to the left
Or if I go to the right
I'm afraid your prognosis
Won't be so bright

For I bring along my friends,
All clones like me
Your liver, your breast,
Your kidney
Are my homes, you see

"Metastasis!"
Says the man with degree

David Berkowitz
October 16, 1989

Corn Stalk

The corn stalk
Stands tall not rigid
Swayed by a tender breeze
One thin stem it stands on
Leaning north or south with ease

But man is most unyielding
And won't bend on his two stems
Yet they both will wither
And wilt down to the ground

The man he fades to ashes
The corn just fades to brown

David Berkowitz
Oct. 17, 1989

Swamp Sojourner
(In Early Winter)

My soul wanders silently
through this swampy meadow,
while flakes of snow
whirl and settle
about my feet.

Saddened that
no life is stirring,
sleep has come
to my friends
in their dens.

Solitude amidst
a million straws
of swamp grass,
all frozen solid
as if under a
sorcerer's spell.

I too have sought
this place to sojourn,
to soothe my weary mind.

These creatures of the swamp,
they sleep more soundly than I.
They've made their beds
in sheltered places,
warmed by the heat of
their own bodies,
secluded in their
remote sanctuaries.

What arcane secrets
can they reveal to me
about survival
while I struggle to live
in a harsh and pitiless
world of men?

David Berkonz
October 20, 1989

Goodnight, My Son

(A Prisoner's Thoughts About His Little Son)

Goodnight, my son
Goodnight, my son
Have sweet and pleasant
Dreams

A watchful eye
i'll keep for thee,
Tho I'm far away,
It seems

Goodnight, my son
Sleep tight, my son
May serenity
come to thee

many miles away
I linger, thinking
of you and me
Oh, if this could be
. . . . .

I'd like to be free
one day, as free
As a bird in flight,
To hold you, hug you,
Kiss your cheek,
And wish you a pleasant
Goodnight

Daniel Berkowitz
October 22, 1989

God's Avenger

What is it you see out that window
For you sit here everyday
Gazing out upon the town
Like a sailor by the bay?

"What grandeur lies before me,
What splendor for my eyes,
To see this town weeping,
Weeping before it dies!"

Why do you slouch so, shoulders
Sagging, stiff - you so silent,
Hushed like a broken bell,
What sights do you see,
can you tell?

"I watch the digger in the graveyard,
His spade sounds the dread alarm,
That this town to sunset
Shall vanish and be gone."

But why should it vanish?
Why should it die?
For this is a wonderful little township
For weary travellers to stop by—
And I see no one weeping,
Nor a tear from any eye.

"Ah, this town is blasphemous,
'Tiz no place for a saint with crown,
The travellers, they wear bluejeans,
And our ladies,
Their petticoats are
Too quick to fall down.

David Berkowitz
October 27, 1989

Warsaw, 1940's

Do you remember Mendelsohn?
His cigar smelling like manure,
That odorous scent—
And ashes on his living room floor
With his scolding wife
On hands and knees scrubbing
Now all are ashes:
Cigar, Mendelsohn, wife
Scattered in the wind

And whatever became of Gittlestein?
His gold teeth glimmering in the
Twilight of his darkroom,
That little photography store
Where people came to store
At wilted-yellow photos
From ancient affairs
(bar mitzvahs, weddings)
Of years gone by—

Golden teeth like the molten sun
At sunset now sit
On a soldier's mantlepiece
Over a crackling fire
Screaming for their owner—
Oh, if those teeth could talk!

And Rabinowitz the cantor?
Where's his voice now with that
Familiar chorus of singing relatives—
Rabinowitz with wife Rebecca
Sung their last line out of tune
With fellow countrymen
In a small cubicle
Not fit for ten yet
Filled with thirty souls—

Staccato screams riddling Rabinowitz
With notes and noises the cantor
Never heard in his fifty years—
A short life now sleeping
With only the memories
Of songs of sorrows
And lamentations
and mournings
And no one
To say
Kaddish

David Berkowitz
October 29, 1989

65

The Journey

Its over now
The waiting
Departure and
Preparation for
The journey
That scores
Have made
Since when
Man came

A Journey
Into something
Dark or light
The sea or
Meadows of
Golden grass
A Journey
Made by
All

Daniel Berkowitz
October 30, 1989

To Robert Frost

He travelled a winding road,
and trod on arduous trail.
But when he could
He gladly would
Detour to tell a tale.

Daniel Berkowitz
Nov. 1, 1989

Robert Frost Says "Goodnight"

My pen was my sword.
Words, the battle cry
of how I thought
I should fight.
I've said hello.
Now I'll say goodnight.

David Berkowitz
Nov. 1, 1989

Robert Frost Runs Out of Ink

The inkwell's empty now;
it could use a refill.
So con my quill.
This pen has run dry
After years of scribbling
And nibbling at
Words in the by and by.

David Berkowitz

Nov. 1, 1989

Bedtime Wishes

Lay me gentle
Lay me down
Into my fine pine
Bed in the ground—
A garland of roses
For my crown—
A white silken
Dress woven around
A satiny ringed
Velvet gown—
Purple lilacs
From the town—
A host of fallen leaves
The color of brown
Blanket me as I hide

Under a dark clay mound—
A covered chamber
Devoid of sound
where I sleep bound
Still and tight
With bones bleached white
Ah, goodnight!

David Berkowitz
November 3, 1989

I AM NO WITCH

Today I went before the elders of the church -
Mean, unmerciful men who never considered consultation;
They only wanted a confession, which I wouldn't give,
For I had nothing to confess
And having pled my case, I can only contend,   5
That they have conspired against me,
And will not cease until I am churning
And burning on a stake.

Suffice to say, I practice no Craft, but only
Sew clothes and scrub floors for my wages.   10
Furthermore, I state that I am no witch-
Not I. I've no power to make a housebroom
Fly. That broom there, the one in the corner,
It's only for sweeping and it can't do much
Else.   15

Mister Swenson? I didn't cause him to die.
He was an everyday drunkard who'd use any
Excuse to buy rum. He died a miserable bum,
And his tankard helped to make the day go by.

The Hansen's hens? I didn't cause them to lie   20
Barren without eggs. Who knows what they've
Been fed. Bread which the spirits cursed.
Its not the worst thing that's happened to
Them. They've never been blessed.

Now Mabel Wheeler, that was a mess,   25
When her husband Harold keeled over, and
Fell off his horse and poked out an eye.
But he was the laziest kind of guy,
And oftentimes he'd fall asleep under
The hay.   30
Its my guess, if I may say,
That those rats, the big ones that
Look like dogs, killed Mrs. Cass's cats.
I've never done evil to any of them.
And Mrs. Cass is so chuff and vulgar, too.   35

Who? Who put a tarantula n Thelma Throop's bed?
Sorcerers! Someone whose head was filled
With hatred for Throop.
Why it could have been a group
Of persons who like tarot cards   40
And those who tamper with the elemental
Forces. Besides, Thelma had few friends.

Fools are those who tamper with witch's tools.
But I've no use for potions or lotions, formulas
And herbs, chamomile or darnel grass, or passion   45
Flowers.

The hours tick by as I wait for a verdict. In this
Dungeon, righteous nuns perched above in a guard tower,
Glower at me with hopes that I'd confess. But to
What? They've even searched under my dress   50
For signs: a pimple? A witch's mark?
Nothing!

Yet I pace and pace. Nuns stop to study
My face as if a wrinkle will reveal my guilt.
Yet I declare, I am no witch. Not, not I.   55
I can't make milk out of lye. And I cannot
Make an imp to lie next to me for sex.
A hex? I've cast not a one. Not even for fun,
Or play. As I've said before I have no power
To make a broom fly.   60
You see that broom over there? The one in
The corner of this little courtyard. Now if
I were really a witch, I'd make it fly. I'd
Hop on and be gone like a raven sailing in
The sky. Just watch me. See, I'm throttling   65
This broom. Bye, bye……………
……………

David Berkowitz

November 6, 1989

NATURE RECLAIMS

The wind persevered and has destroyed
A house where lived a family.
Where are they now? Shall they
Claim the land, or allow the wind
To reclaim it for Nature?
For once there were four,
But one by one, each walked
Through Death's door.
And the house alone in this valley,
Stands stark and still-
Silently giving testimony to
Nature's victory.
For day by day the wood erodes
And beams lean forward tilting.
Each creak that's heard tells the tale
Of a house, abandoned, slowly wilting.
As the wind whips up and stirs
The valley, an empty house
Speaks hauntingly by whistling,
The voice of the wind through gapping
Holes, says for Nature the word
"Submission."
A house once standing strong and proud,
Is now seen bending to its knees in
Contrition.
As Nature takes back what was hers,
In slow, never-slackening
Retaliation.

David Berkowitz

November 28, 1989

NATURE BECKONS OUR RETURN

Who is one such as I
Who keeps pace with all the seasons,
Who greets the sparrows with kindness
And calls them all my teachers.
Aren't they?
For Nature has a say
To reach her creatures,
Those who've gone astray-
Like us humans who've lost
Our way,
And been choked by commerce,
And lured by the clanging chimes
Of cash registers that sing treason,
Or schools that don't
Teach the reasons
Why men must pay attention
To the seasons.

David Berkowitz

December 12, 1989

KILL DAY

Thee was nothing but smoldering stubble and rubble. Here stood rows upon rows of trees all roasted battlefield black after barrages of bombings and shellings. Gnarled branches looked like outstretched hands reaching out from flaming buildings, pleading, as if they could be saved.

Slowly the boys were marching, mumbling and cursing under their breath, damning God and the Germans for their misery. While the earth, its dead-like crust caused soldier boots to make crunching noises. And a crackling of twigs. Oh God, twigs!

Stopping stunned, Sergeant Stephenson, the platoon leader, strained and grimaced upon receipt of a signal from across the valley. Rapidly spinning around to face his charges, he said, quite poetically, although not intending to be: "Step over so lightly boys, through this field of muck and slime. Soldier scouts report the sight of a mine. And there's usually more than one. Yes, many…Tiptoe, tiptoe. No time to twaddle or prattle. Boys, the slightest ripple, rustle or rattle will send those watchdogs into battle."

Now the mines, like steel sentinels they sat, always alert for the trespassers foot, anxious to place their metal pats into some hapless soldier.

The sergeant continued with his instructions: "And for godsakes, don't even dare to wink an eye because those Bett's will surely blow us into the sky. I don't want to have to tell your folks back home that I watched you die. So stay still and just lie. Don't even think, boys, don't even think. For surely they'll dispatch us into the firmament."

Shivering like marmots on a chilly jungle morning, a platoon of soldiers stood waiting, crouched low, as if somehow - if they'd just stall for a few minutes, those mines would disappear. But they weren't going to. Having stood guard for several years, well camouflaged under a collection of twigs and branches on the valley floor, these mechanical killers were just itching for the chance to prove themselves worthy of their reputations.

The fatherly Sergeant Stephenson, gathering his gear in the ready to move on, warned: "Pray no one be so foolish to flinch or flutter, or even utter a single sound. For we'll all be minced meat in the ground. Step lightly. Step down. Easy boys, easy. Don't make a sound. And watch those damn twigs!"

But the mines wee in no hurry. The had no place to go, no home or appointments. Only that death vigil. This was all they were required to keep. And faithful they were. Listening. Trying to count how many men were out there traversing the woods, zigzagging towards them. Heavy breathing, Heaving. Vibrations from the ceaseless beatings of soldier hearts. Would today be their day to kill? To greet the soldiers with sharp shrapnel-like strips of shredded metal?

Stephenson's platoon slowly meandered through tangles of swamp weeds and rotten bark. But a sudden unexpected cackling of a suprised wild bird sent those dozen scared soldiers scurrying for cover, diving to hid. And a crackling of twigs! The stomping of feet! The sergeant yelled: "Shut up! Stand still, you bloody sissies! One wrong move and we'll all be missing legs and heads, our bones like broken eggs!"

Stephenson, a wizened old soldier with his oft crude philosophical bent that only yeas of war and misery could mold, reeled to his men and shouted: "Who'll call out cadences for Death? Who'll announce the Reaper's grim toll? Who'll go home in a coffin, and who'll live to grow old?"

It seemed like such a silly thing to say; this self-appointed philosopher and uneducated poet in a war zone. But seconds later, Sergeant Stephenson answered his own questions.

You see, there was a twig there among lots of twigs. Oh, it was just an ordinary looking twig. However, if you looked at it more closely, which that old soldier didn't do, he would have seen that twig step out from among his companions. And if he would have only listened, as if a twig could talk and one could hear it, he would have heard it say: "Go ahead. Step on me. I dare you." But he didn't hear, and he stepped.

David Berkowitz

January 5, 1990

THE TEMPLE OF THE NIGHT

Howls of laughter
And cries of delight,
Woo the faithful to
The Temple of the Night.

Bowls of Joy
And a twinkling of glasses,
Lure the faithful
To the entrance passes.

A grinning of gin
And a toasting of rum
Bid the faithful to enter,
The thirsty to come.

A chalice lifted to
Cracked, parched lips-
Lovely pleasures for
Lonely souls.

Dancing shadows in dimly
Lit aisles, inspire the
Faithful with gentle
Sighs and cries.

Like an old witch toils
Over her kettles and pots,
The Brew Master gathers
His bottles of hops.

Bubbles dance and dew drops
Spring from golden cups
Oak scented casks
Of perfumed vintage crops.
Drink deep, acolyte friend,
And quench the fire that
In dire hours of need
Consumes the souls of men.

May 20, 1990*

*Rev. Aug. 14, 1990

THE JUMPER

I stood studying your frame
as crimsoned stains seeped
onto the pavement floor,
slow spreading liquid red
tentacles that seemed to
encircle you, as if to cut
off the escape of your soul.
Your arms, like broken wings,
lie outstretched as if they
were trying to catch
the wind.
Crooked hands, with fingers
cupped, caress cold concrete.
Bent kneeling, bowed over
your flight has taken from you
the bitterness that was your life.
An ear sunk below the surface,
tour clothing splattered,
your body like a cup that's
been dropped and shattered.
Who were you but a loner
among men, unknown, like
a fallen soldier in the war
against despair. Now a life-
less heap that, even in death
your crumbled corpse rests like
a monument to those whose dreams
have died.

David Berkowitz

June 9, 1990

NOWHERE

(A Poem About Vietnam)

Right in the middle of Nowhere
I stand frozen on a hot humid night.
A night so dark that its blackness
envelopes my every pore making me
gasp for air.

Silently, motionlessly, I stand
listening for any suspicious sound.
But a chorus of crickets chirp incessantly
drowning out all other noises except for
the sudden startling rustle of a scurrying
animal as it brushes up against some bushes
in its search for food.

Yet I search too, and scan the forest floor
for my foe whom I always watch for but seldom
get a chance to see except for, maybe a fleet-
ing glimpse as he, like the fur creatures of
the jungle, scampers off at my boot sounds
or scent or both. A sixth sense like a
tiger's, he's always one step out of
reach.

Such is my poor luck as I compete my skills
against his. His sniper/sapper sophistication
deceives me daily as I see my friends fall
one by one from his clever devices.

Its hopeless, really. The boom boom explosions
of artillery and the clack crack blowing of
Claymores slay nothing but birds and trees.
I'm getting tired of this game of Swift vs. Swifter
while across the sea a Corvette and a cake await
my return; my Corvette sitting idle, my Mom's
fresh baked cake getting cold like the corpses
of my friends.

I'm only nineteen and certainly not a philosopher.
But what I do know is that, for me this could be my
last day on earth. Hours ago I may have witnessed
my last sunset. The ancient axiom "Live and let live"
has died along with the day. If I had to perish I'd
rather do it with Moma at my side than out here in
Nowhere.

David Berkowitz

June 19, 1999

TRAPPED IN A NEW YORK CITY APARTMENT

Trapped and entombed behind a locked and bolted
steel door with chains that snake this way and
that, you sit frozen in fear. Startled by an
unfamiliar sound, you jump up gripping your
sofa with sweaty palms.
Screeching cats and scratching rats slink
passed your barred window, staring in at
you with malicious intent.
Sirens in the night howl warnings to you
that Death is stalking the streets.
And you, watching the clock, wait
desperately for the sunrise, that
signal from the Divine that its now
safe to come out and shop.

Daniel Berkowitz

June 20, 1990

B-52

Here I am, a metallic death machine
flying high above the forest floor.
Like Michael the Archangel, I declare
war from the heavens. And I rain fire
and brimstone as my judgments upon the
earth.
With the grace of a large silver scythe
swung from the invisible hands, I swoop down
and cut to pieces all the things hidden and
exposed, above and below.
I claim al life and lace my prey
eagerly into the hands of the
Eternal Reaper.
My scythe slices and severs both men
and trees as everything that breathes
is mine for the slaughter.
From my angelic hands I drip red hot
sheets of fire so as to purify and
purge the land of every creature,
be it fair of foul.
My enemies smolder beneath my feet.
Their screams silenced by an angry roar
as I come to conquer, creating a fine
mixture of blood and earth soil.
Sinners behold, a splendid smite
I render to the unprepared and unwary.
My calling card is a charred and cratered
ground. I topple kingdoms and cities,
and I create destruction and re-create
a barren earth.

David Berkowitz

June 29, 1990

SPEAKING FROM SOWETO

The capitalists have left us crushed and destitute while Poverty's cruel clutch and its continual shame has seared our souls with despair.

Our cooking pots re empty and our pants pockets have invisible holes that eat our last few coins.

This city is nothing but a string of mud hovels, rat conduits, really. And our homes are connected by chasms of rotting garbage; heaps of trash like the expanse of the sea spill out into the horizon.

The hollowed faces of our children peak from cracks in the walls as Prosperity eludes their fathers' workless hands.

We have no clean children here to chase dreams, no trees with outstretched limbs extended into endless welcomes. Instead we have weeds slipping through dirt mound cracks, struggling to survive like we do in Soweto.

David Berkowitz

June 30, 1990

VIRUS

Bathing in brothels
with my gracious host,
I am a guest unseen,
uninvited.
Sometimes traveling
from city to city,
coast to coast,
as I ride
the pleasure circuit,
bringing pain
at the end of
life's road.

Like the devil,
who does his dirty work
in darkness,
I slip unannounced
through a carelessly unguarded
open back door,
leaving me to explore
a pitch-black cavern,
as I look to make
my abode among
fellow thieves.

A forever hunter,
I'll hound and wound
my prey
until Eternity
tells me
to stop sucking away
my host's slowly ebbing
lifeforce.
Like Romeo and Juliet,
we are locked in our
last death embrace.
My poisoned host
left to suffer disgrace,
for he must come
face to face
with his many
mortal sins.

Yet the two of us,
like lovers clinging,
share each others bodies
while we await the cleansing,
absolving pyre.

Daniel Berkowitz

July 9, 1990

HOMELESS, GO HOME

Homeless, go home, hide!
We don't want you here,
so close, so near
that we could see
your shame.
We don't want to hear
your cries of hunger
coming from cracked,
parched lips
begging us for crumbs,
like Lazarus
longing to be fed
bread and droppings
with our dogs
living better
than you do.

David Berkowitz

July 15, 1990

THE BATTLE OF THE SOMME

Sweat drenched and dirty
from dozens upon dozens of endless days of dread,
as Death sweeps away all time, seasons and men
in a spray of bullets -
battalions at full-speed charge Fusiliers forward,   5
trigger ready, refusing concealment,
as they attempt to penetrate enemy lines.
Yet gain no ground as round upon round of artillery,
beat them backwards into bunkers built like catacombs,   10
six feet deep, crammed with souls -
shells pound the surface,
while German gunners,
groaning with ammo loads,
rush to fill the stomachs
of hungry cannons.   15

In bunkers below ground,
lay or boys smothering in dust -
the icons of parents
pulled out at prayer time -
while thundering rumbles of shells   20
tumble men in their tracks.
In trenches, flag banners blessed
by priests before departure, fly low
as sharpshooters seek to delete our numbers
and add to Sheol's toll.   25

German soldiers, from sunrise to sunset
speak to us fro the barrels of Mausers
and Maxim machineguns, while we await
the charge-call bugles and choruses
of Vickers to cheer us onward.   30
Multitudes of men near naked
as biting strands of barbed wire
steal shirts off backs, and mudholes,
sucking us to knees, snatch boots from feet.
Yet barefoot,   35
We run up sludge hills of blood and mud -
piles of steel helmets riddled with holes,
lie like markers forewarning.
But brave fools press forward
amid the dyings' calling cries   40

In the Somme, summer splays the landscape
with greens, and birds sing of peace
in the carnage, calling truce.
Doves and wild pigeons coo love songs
to mates in shrubs,   45

85

oblivious to soldiers whose hate
lays waste the valley,
while battles rage in trenches
and along stalemated front lines.

Yet in England, in later years,   50
the November bells
tell lullabies to the war weary,
announcing Armistice and asking why,
four hundred thousand thousand of our boys
now lie under the Somme's setting sun.   55

David Berkowitz

July 17, 1990

BOWERY BUM

I watched you wander
downcast through cold
damp streets to squander
your coins on cheap wine.
A hulk of soulless man
in an doorway huddled,
in a cloak of rags bundled
to ward off the
merciless whipping wind
that, by early dawn,
will have you whittled
into a frozen corpse
fit only for a nameless
plot in Potter's Field.

David Berkowitz

September 6, 1990

HARLEM HOOKERS

Who are these night prowling
glittering girls lined in rows
with their backs against buildings,
like caricatures of scarecrows?
These drug stupor sleepless slaves   5
stagger drunk-like after strangers.
Haunted hollow-eyed lookers -
carnival clown painted faces,
the Harlem street hookers.
With stale perfume traces,   10
they slip past like zombies -
some stoned on crack -
all of them junkies.
Yet they have the knack
at displaying their charms -   15
platinum head hustling harlots -
their scarred swollen arms
track the number of their days
selling their souls for pay
while marking a path   20
to Death's doorstep.

David Berkowitz

September 9, 1990

SLOWLY

I remember your pain; its
twisting, turning, churning through
your body, burning you like hot fire
deep within your bosom.
It never seemed to end.   5
It would rend you senseless,
Delirious and screaming.
What moans and agony!
The pain made you writhe
like a madwoman out of control,   10
contorted face grimacing.

Within months all that was left
of your face was bloatedness; only
two strands of grey white hair left
on your head, oily.   15
For want of a bath
you swam in excrement,
bedpan always overflowing.
What a way to die.
Not quickly like some, mercifully.   20
Slowly. To make you cry.
Slowly.

Who invented this torture?
Surely a madman who loves pain.
In bed hour after hour looking   25
at a sea of nurses slipping in
and out, silently like the tide;
like the changing of the guard.
Night shift. Day shift.
They just let you rot into a corpse.   30

Slowly. Always slowly. Creeping
towards death but never quickly
getting there. See you, I'd
never wish cancer on anyone.

David Benkowitz

November 13. 1990

89

GRAND CANYON

A canyon so vast -
It doesn't seem to have
A beginning or ending.
How can one grasp
What its like to stand
Looking north, east,
South, west into eternity.
Attuned to nature,
Aware that I'm just a speck,
Like a sand particle empty
Of mind and powerless -
This canyon humbled me,
Showed me that its
Brown baked walls will
Outlast me. Millions
Of years before I was born,
Millions of years after I'm gone,
These dry sandstone cliffs
Will live on,
Forgetting me.

David Berkowitz

December 11, 1990

<u>ONCE</u>

ONCE I ran the hills breathless for endless hours,
shooting through tall grass and flowers,
zigzagging past pine trees and elm,
a boundless passion -
cells charged with life,   5
and heart fire of youth
burning liquid red.
Who thought it would ever end.
Not me. Not suddenly
in the middle of a dream.   10

ONCE laughter danced around me
like a flower in full bloom
future thoughts stood like torches
lighting the way for many tomorrows.

ONCE sorrow was not a word,   15
for I only saw pets die or animals -
little furry things that
would lie in the roadway stretched flat,
anonymous and stinking.
But this was all once, and long ago.   20
For by surprise, and suddenly,
two bright lights sprung upon me
on a dark country road
illuminating everything.
Then in an instant   25
I was thrown into
everlasting exile from the living.

David Berkowitz

December 13, 1990

SO LONG, JERK

It was like a metamorphosis
When you left our offices
The place became tranquil
Co-workers were thankful
Projects got done
We actually had fun

We prayed and prayed
That you'd get laid
Off, and off you went
Unemployed and silent
Now its back to work
Minus one useless jerk

Daniel Berkowitz

December 24, 1990

18TH CENTURY SOLDIER'S BALLARD

Through summer's endless sunlight,
And autumn's early fall,
Through winter's cold twilight
And spring's early call,
We dragged our carcass heavy,
Lugged cannons and ball,
Over mountains and down valleys,
Through rain, sleet and squall,
All to answer the battle call.

Though our burdens may be many
And our rewards be small and slim,
We live by luck and grace of God,
Trusting totally in Him.

David Berkowitz

December 26, 1990

DISABLED

I've seen a legless beggar
Humbled o his stumps
Tin can hand outstretched,
Hoping for quarters or dimes.

Stopped to talk to him once,
And learned he was a Vet.
A Vietcong booby trap took
One-third of him in a flash.

Our government, in turn,
Gave him few opportunities
To honestly earn some cash.

At night I see him rummaging
Through endless piles
Of New York City's trash.

Daniel Berkowitz

July 1, 1991

JUDAS*

"Hail Rabbi,
King of the Jews!"
I've sold you for silver,
that's the bad news.

I'm the slayer betrayer
who seized you with kiss.
I've spilt innocent blood,
and I can't live with this.

The Field of Blood
became my grave,
my soul with guilt
you will not save.

So hang I will
from the highest tree,
swinging by rope
into eternity.

January 2, 1991

*Judas Iscariot betrayed Jesus with a kiss. For leading the chief priests and elders to Him, Judas was given thirty pieces of silver. However, filled with guilt, he went back to the Jewish priests to return the coins. They, according to the Biblical account, refused to accept the silver back because it was given for the "price of blood." Instead they purchased a small field, a Potter's Field, I which to bury poor strangers and unknowns. According to legend, till this day it is called the "Field of Blood."

MORNING MEDITATION

In the early morning hours
Before the dew leaves the flowers
As mountain mists lift from the earth,
Before the dawn sun leaps from her berth -
A Path is now open for meditation,
Concentration, Reflection, Contemplation.

Before the birds rise from their nests,
It's the perfect time if one invests
In yoga and deep breathing
Leaving one's cares and one's grieving
To that past world, a world
Filled with despair, and embroiled
In hatred, bitterness and strife
That will quickly end your life.

The early morn is best for me,
A continuity of cycles since eternity -
The fading stars and pale moon
Blend with the coming soon
Of sun and birds and flowers -
The heat of long daylight hours.

You see, the dawn is really a time of rest
And one who understands this is truly blest.
In the quiet center of one's mind
And in the heart of Nature you will find,
An invitation from the sun,
To rise to greet it before the day's begun.
For what Nature has in store
Is to help us, heal us, and so much more.

David Barkowitz

January 5, 1991

"WORMWOOD"

(Revelation, Chapter 8)

Sea: what have you become
But a corrosive cauldron
Heated by the scorching sun.
Cadavers of fish float
With the tide,
Their silver scales surface
And bob under the dancing feet
Of a thousand thousand flies.

Scavenger sea gulls
Poke their rusty beaks
Through layers of scum
Searching for food.
Swells of oil ooze and
Slime drift seawards.
Flotsam bobs over breakers,
Drifts towards shore,
Channels and inlets smother
As mussels and snails choke
On fresh filtered trash.
Another woe is here.
Another woe has passed.
The waters re cursed.
And the sea which gives us life,
Has given us her dead instead.
"Wormwood" has crashed,
Has fallen into the sea,
And the bitterness of the waters,
Like the bitter blood,
Has killed one third
Of mankind.

David Berkowitz

January 5, 1991

87 DEAD IN A SOUTH BRONX
SOCIAL CLUB FIRE

Choking smoke curled quickly
Around a hundred pairs of hands,
With fingers clawing blindly
Against a sea of swirling black clouds.

Coal black clouds   5
That charged upon the unsuspecting,
Suddenly in a rush -
A smothering whirlwind.

Dancing feet broke into a run.
Bouncing bodies rammed into walls   10
As the only path of escape
Was possessed by sheets of flame.

Whose to blame them for their screams?
Sharp shrill screams of terror
That bore into everyones ears   15
With a burning heat,
Deafening, unrelenting until
The smoke clouds
Slipped into the night sky.

The dance ended with the perished   20
Huddled in piles. Puddles
Of Holy ash water
Soaked their garments brown.

Soot stained stone dead faces
Stared upwards at a ceiling   25
Of peeling paint. Yet they
Were beyond feeling pain.
The mourners gathered quickly.
By sunrises a stunned crowd,
Thronged by disbelief,   30
Jammed the streets to peer
At white sheeted wet corpses
Laid out to dry in the early sun.

Stark blank faces stood rigid.
And those made insane by loss   35
Tossed themselves upon the sidewalk
With walls of despair.
In tiny apartments,
Houschold patron saints
Their statue images standing guard,   40

Stayed silent and refused
To protect those who
Left their houses for the pyre party
That night.

But who really knew   45
That Death would dance
At the club that day?
By whom was he invited?

In the aftermath
A building stands burnt black,   50
Locked and vacant -
Empty except for the hollow ghosts
Of the South Bronx dead.

David Berkowitz

January 8, 1991

<u>RICH AND POOR</u>

In posh restaurants
Amidst sparkling lights
And dazzling glitter,
Food gatherers gorge
On ample fare.

On streets outside
Hungry paupers grab
For stale rolls
And greats grub
From trash receptacles.

What a spectacle of
Rich and poor divided.
"tough times never last,"
Goes the saying.
They just go on forever.

David Berkowitz

July 4, 1991

STOMPING GROUND

(The Death of a Homeless Man)

They swam in the dimly lit tunnel
Like a school of piranha in a stench-filled pond.
Seeking a mal of bloody flesh.
When they spotted him,
A crumbled heap in
Slumbering sleep,
Snoring oblivious in his
Drunken dream world,
A world that amounted
To as much as his life -
Nothing!

They circled his wrinkled frame,
Pulses racing, breathing deep,
Excited at the anticipation
Of the kill.

Then it began swiftly
As if on cue.
Left, right.
Left, right.
Left, right.
Steel-tipped commando boots
Cracked ribs.
A frenzy of fists
Plummeted flesh
Until death set in.
Backing away
From the silent heap
That was once a human life,
Only the sounds of heavy breathing
Could be heard.

For some moments
They stood over the corpse
Surveying. Satisfied.
Slowly they turned away
Into the night, traveling
Back through the tunnel
Into darkness.

In the morning rush
He was found
Slumped and down.
At first he was
Mistaken for a pile

Of discarded trash,
A clump of clothing
At the far end of the
Tunnel.

On the subway platform
Lay a discarded beggar.
Homeless.
A no name
To be tossed out
With the morning trash.
And in New York City,
Piranha-like youths prowl
And kill for fun.

David Berkowitz

April 28, 1992

A BEDTIME AFFAIR

What is it I adore
that lays hidden inside
your heart?
That sweet nectar,
a fragrance of mint
and spice.
So arousing and pleasant.
You are an aphrodisiac,
a lover filled with dark
kisses.

At night I will
invite you into my bed.
Just the two of us
locked in an embrace,
your joy running down
my face.

It is true that you won't
cheat on me.
But I will cheat,
oh yes,
on my diet.

Perhaps this box
of Valentine's chocolates
is the best love there is!

David Berkowitz

April 25, 1992

STUPID HOUSE PAINTER

Stupid house painter,
His spray speckled face
A blank like his brain.
Calculating with his brush,
Counting bristles into the night.
A rush of endless strokes--
Up, down, up, down, up, down…
Swiping around clocks,
Scraping spills from floors.
A wife and seven kids
Sit waiting with supper.
While tired stained hands
Wash themselves in benzene.
How much money will he make?
Not much!
How long will it take
To paint 100,000 blank walls?
A lifetime!

David Berkowitz

May 19, 1992

SHOE SHINE BOY

Shoe Shine Boy,
Age fifty-five.
Professional servant.
His scuff stained hands
Carries a wooden box
Throughout Midtown.

Open for business anyplace.
Fifty cents for a quickie.
One dollar for a quality shine.
Plus tip, please.

Counting quarters for carfare home.
What a way
To earn a living
New York style!

David Berkowitz

May 20, 1992

WE RE PRISONERS

WE ARE
As babies crying
For mother's
Long dead.

WE ARE
As children crying
For fathers
Gone to graves.

WE ARE
The ghosts
Of dreams
That died.

WE ARE
The prisoners
Of our
Own hands.

WE ARE
The killers
Of ourselves.

David Berkowitz

September 13, 1993

<u>IN FOREVER</u>

WE SHUT
> the doors
>> of hope.

WE LOCKED
> ourselves in,
>> and now
>>> we can't
>>>> get out.

David Berkowitz

September 14, 1993

THE PRISON YARD: SUMMER

WE ARE AS
clay pots
baked brittle
under summer's
burning sun.

Skin roasted red
darkening dark brown,
dry and stagnant,
and tired.

Empty shells of
men gone sour -
vacant vessels
devoid of soul.

The prison yard:
a desolate sea
of rejected humanity.

A place
filled with
lonely men.

David Berkowitz

Sept. 14, 1993

The Angry Young Lions

by David Berkowitz

The Lions sit meekly in their cages
Held now in captivity after a
Lifetime spent hunting their prey
In the jungles of concrete and glass
Wasting away the remainder of their
Days
Staring at fluorescent lightbulbs in
The ceiling.

Lion tamers, dozens of them,
Strutting about with clubs,
Seeking to tame these wild beasts
Fearful of being mauled
Hating their charges.

Angry young Lions
Most in the prime of life
Full of power and strength
Locked in a cage

Angry
Hungry
Full of murderous rage
Having to walk in single file
When once

They roamed free
But without purpose
Roaming the open roads
Preying upon others
Others preying upon them
In jungles full of concrete and glass
Taking their freedom for granted.

But then capture!
Arrest and incarceration!

Now the Lions sit in cages
One by one
Under the watchful eyes
Of their tamers
Whose job it is
To re-orientate and re-educate
The beasts

with force if necessary
To teach them how to live
In the jungles
Without stalking and killing
To live honestly
In a dishonest world
To teach them virtues
In a virtueless world
To teach them principles
In a world where
Principles are nonexistent
where governments are corrupt
And politicians steal
And those with money
Can kill their prey
without having to be stained
with its blood.

Angry Young Lions
Bewildered and confused
In a violent world
All their lives
Surviving by wit

And courage
And instinct
Now held captive
By those who fear them
Yet waiting for the day
When the tamers must meet
And decide
And determine
That these Lions are
No longer dangerous
That they no longer
Will seek live game
But will gladly settle
For a bowl of lettuce
And will willingly revert
To a passive existence
That is as alien to them
Is the lives of their keepers.

David Berkowitz

A Memorial Out of Place
by David Berkowitz

Its a small park in the South Bronx that is primarily used as a hangout for winos and junkies. Surrounded by housing projects and tenements, its pavement covered by broken glass, it occassionally serves as an oasis for the neighborhood kids who sometimes play handball and basketball there.

Located at the corner of Willis Avenue and East 135th Street, just off the Major Deegan Expressway, it goes by the name of Carlos Lozada park. For the addicts and kids that use the park, the name Carlos Lozada probably has no significance. But for the members of the 173d Airborne Brigade (Airmobile) who served in Vietnam, and more specifically, who fought in the battle of Hill 875 during the Fall season of 1967, the name carries great weight.

The park is named in memory of Carlos, a former Bronx resident, who died on Hill 875 fighting for his country. But he was no ordinary soldier. On November 19, 1967, he single-handedly killed 25 Vietcong soldiers with his M-60 machine gun in what Army officials said was some of the most bitter fighting in the war. And for his bravery and courage, he was awarded (posthumously) the nation's highest award — the Medal of Honor.

Carlos Lozada is survived by his wife Linda (who never remarried) and his daughter Yvette. For them, Carlos is more than a name tacked onto a rundown, dilapidated city park. For Linda he once meant life and hope, and maybe even an escape from the slums. She still has his letters and rereads them often. Her daughter was too young to even remember him.

Perhaps by dedicating this park to him, government officials will feel that they've absolved themselves of any guilt in his death. Who knows?

But the least we could do is to recognize the sacrifices and contributions that each veteran has made, be it loss of life or limb. For Carlos Lozada, his memorial is far removed from the Vietnam Veterans War Memorial in Washington, D.C. Its far removed from the crowds, parades, and fanfare. No government officials go to Lozada park, and no fancy ceremonies are held there. For his memorial is too far out of place. But the spirit of this brave paratrooper lives on.

- End -

At Rest In Greenwood

Jennie Franco

My short years wrap me like a cloth
of schooldays, feast days, my First Communion dress.
The cord of mornings, stitching at Triangle
up in the loft before light.

I trace the thread to my last, my fifteenth birthday.
Ribbons of friends dance the Tarantella,
circling plates of tortoni and ices
out on our stoop after dark.

And Mama says, don't forget Our Lady
and always light a holy candle on your birthday.
Today she twists rosary beads between my ruined fingers,
plaits roses in my veil.

Neighbors nail flowers, black crepe
to the doors, they have covered my face
with lilies and forget-me-nots.
I am circled with tapers.

I rest in the front room
next to the room where I was born.
The brass band wraps up our street,
"Panis Angelicus" stops at our stoop.

The Sons of Italy and Saint Angelo Society
have hired a cart just for my flowers.
Papa says, only the best for our Jennie.
A fine lady, I am lifted into my carriage.

The Grass-harp of hymns follows the line
of Eleventh Street. Inside its woven voice
I know each murmuring Ave Maria.
The sky smells like lilies.

Slower. Silence. We are nearing Triangle.
Now the shock of the skeleton loft
unfolds the tall wall of wailing till
Heaven cracks and tatters, blesses us with rain.

ABOUT THE AUTHOR

Stephen and Kenneth Cender have both spent over a decade in the prison setting with David Berkowitz, and as a result of such close association, came to know David extremely well.

Except for the short introduction, the entire book is the writings of David Berkowitz. It is the authors' wishes that the readers make up their own minds as to who and what David Berkowitz is, or has become.